VIKING LONGBOATS

© Aladdin Books Ltd 1989

Designed and produced by
Aladdin Books Ltd
70 Old Compton Street
London W1V 5PA

Printed in Belgium

First published in the
United States in 1989 by
Gloucester Press
387 Park Avenue South
New York, NY, 10016

Back cover: This Viking tombstone was decorated
with a dragon fighting a snake.

Design David West
Children's Book Design

Editor Catherine Bradley
Picture researcher Cecilia Weston-Baker
Illustrator Tony Smith
Map Alex Pang

The author, Margaret Mulvihill, was born in Ireland and lives in London. She is the author of numerous articles for history magazines and books as well as two novels and a biography.

Library of Congress Cataloging-in-Publication Data

Mulvihill, Margaret.
    Viking longboats/by Margaret Mulvihill.
        p. ch. -- (History highlights)
    Includes index.
    Summary: Describes who the Vikings were, how they built their boats, where they traveled to, and daily life in a Viking household.
    ISBN 0-531-17168-X
    1. Viking ships--Juvenile literature. [1. Vikings.] I. Title.
II. Series: History highlights (New York, N.Y.)
V45.M85 1989
948.022--dc20   89-31565
                                                           CIP
                                                           AC

Contents

VIKING LONGBOATS

GLOUCESTER PRESS

New York · London · Toronto · Sydney

INTRODUCTION

Late in the 8th century people from Scandinavia (now Denmark, Norway and Sweden) went south on raiding parties. This was the beginning of the Viking Age, which lasted until 1100. The word "viking" probably comes either from *vik* or *vig*, the Scandinavian word for a creek or battle. In the summer the sailor-warriors went "a-viking," or roving, across the seas in their wonderfully efficient ships. They searched for treasure to bring home or for new lands to settle on.

Why did these people go a-viking? One explanation was that there wasn't enough land in Scandinavia. Norway is very mountainous, Sweden is covered by thick forests and Denmark has large areas of infertile land. The Norwegians raided and then settled in the Faroe, Orkney, and Shetland islands, Scotland, Ireland, and northwest England. The Danes went to Germany, the Netherlands, France, and eastern England. Meanwhile the Swedes reached down through Russia to the Arab world.

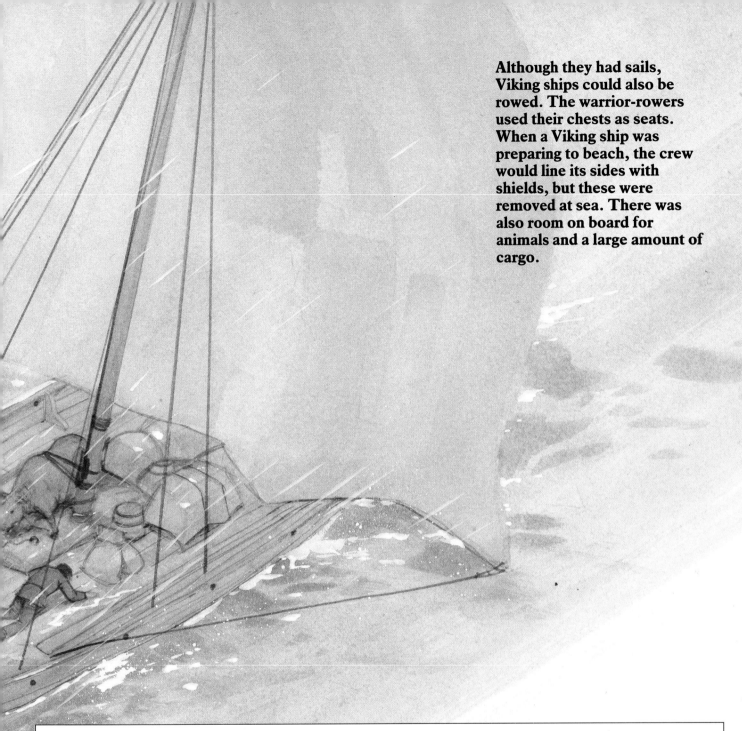

Although they had sails, Viking ships could also be rowed. The warrior-rowers used their chests as seats. When a Viking ship was preparing to beach, the crew would line its sides with shields, but these were removed at sea. There was also room on board for animals and a large amount of cargo.

THE VIKINGS

Norwegian, Swedish and Danish Vikings could all understand each other, even though they spoke different dialects. People thought the Vikings were unusually tall, and the Irish distinguished between them as either dark-haired strangers, the "dubh ghall," or blonde strangers "fionn ghall." The Germans called them ship-men, while the Arabs called them the heathen.

RAIDERS FROM THE SEA

The Vikings were not Christians and saw isolated monasteries and churches as easy targets for hit-and-run raids. In 793 longshipmen attacked the island monastery of Lindisfarne, off northeast England. They destroyed the holy place, took the church treasure, slaughtered some cattle, killed several monks and nuns and took the rest home to be slaves. Soon after these terrible raids were experienced in Ireland, Scotland, Wales, northern England and on the continent of Europe.

Although bows and arrows were used to shoot enemies at long range, Viking soldiers preferred hand-to-hand combat. Some raiders used axes, but more commonly they used spears. Both weapons were used for other purposes: axes could chop timber for houses, and ships and spears could be used for hunting and fishing.

At the time, much of Europe was ruled by Charlemagne, but after his death in 814 his sons quarreled over his empire. They were so busy fighting each other that large inland towns, such as Paris, suffered at the hands of Viking raiders. Monks described the Vikings as "a savage hurricane."

Viking warriors usually wore simple leather caps as helmets. Only the most important men wore armor, such as metal helmets and chain shirts. Vikings took great pride in their weapons but above all they prized their swords. Special swords were handed down through families, and blacksmiths were important members of Viking society.

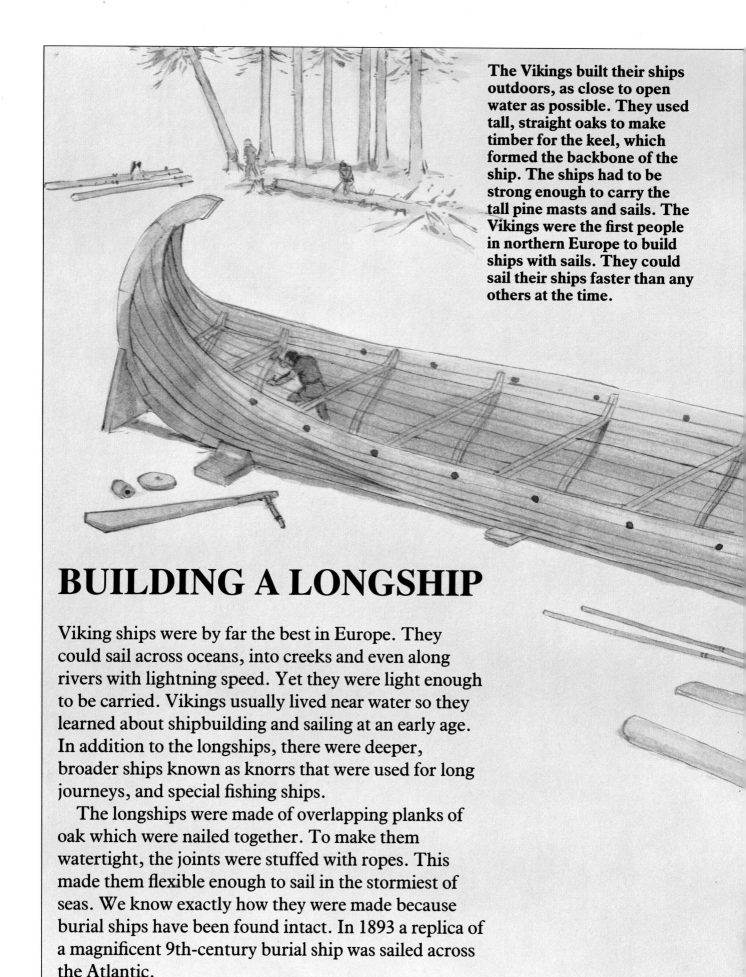

The Vikings built their ships outdoors, as close to open water as possible. They used tall, straight oaks to make timber for the keel, which formed the backbone of the ship. The ships had to be strong enough to carry the tall pine masts and sails. The Vikings were the first people in northern Europe to build ships with sails. They could sail their ships faster than any others at the time.

BUILDING A LONGSHIP

Viking ships were by far the best in Europe. They could sail across oceans, into creeks and even along rivers with lightning speed. Yet they were light enough to be carried. Vikings usually lived near water so they learned about shipbuilding and sailing at an early age. In addition to the longships, there were deeper, broader ships known as knorrs that were used for long journeys, and special fishing ships.

The longships were made of overlapping planks of oak which were nailed together. To make them watertight, the joints were stuffed with ropes. This made them flexible enough to sail in the stormiest of seas. We know exactly how they were made because burial ships have been found intact. In 1893 a replica of a magnificent 9th-century burial ship was sailed across the Atlantic.

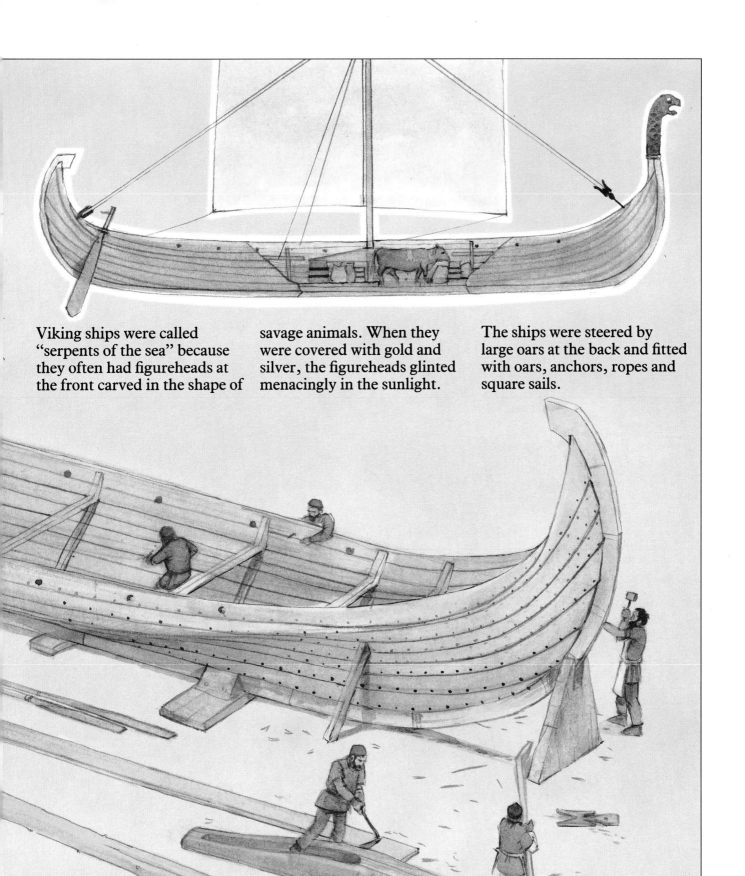

Viking ships were called "serpents of the sea" because they often had figureheads at the front carved in the shape of savage animals. When they were covered with gold and silver, the figureheads glinted menacingly in the sunlight. The ships were steered by large oars at the back and fitted with oars, anchors, ropes and square sails.

TRADING

The wandering Vikings soon became the middlemen of Europe. They took things from the cold north that were valued in the south: furs from sable, fox, squirrel and beaver, dried fish, wood, honey, amber, walrus tusks, walrus hides (for making rope), whale oil, feathers and down for quilts and mattresses. In return Viking merchants brought back wines, spices, silk and silver from the south.

Swedish Vikings traveled down through Russia to Byzantium (now Istanbul). They were interested in Arab silver coins which were valued for their silver content but they also could get hold of goods from the Far East, such as Chinese silk, oriental spices and Persian glass.

The Arabs were fascinated by the Vikings. One writer, Ibn Fadlan, noticed the great size of the "Rus men," their ruddy faces and their fearsome weapons. He also described how vain Viking men were – they loved wearing colorful clothes and precious jewelry. The Byzantine emperor was so impressed by these foreigners that he recruited them into his army to be his Varangian Guard.

Byzantium was a place of great luxury and sophistication. Viking traders were dazzled by the array of goods offered by merchants from Egypt, Moorish Spain, Damascus, Baghdad and even Tashkent. Those who came back were always able to make enormous profits from their visits.

HEADING SOUTH

Swedish Vikings sailed along the Russian rivers, using rollers, when necessary, to transport their ships overland. They went down the Dnieper River to the Black Sea. From there they sailed to Byzantium. Other ships went down the Volga River to the Caspian Sea. While they were in Byzantium, one of the Vikings carved the name "Halfdan" onto a balcony of the Hagia Sophia mosque. The word Russia comes from *rus*, which was a Finnish word for Swedes. Novgorod and Kiev were set up by the Vikings as trading bases. The Vikings also went west to England and France to get wheat, wool, tin, honey and salt.

ENGLAND

Hedeby

FRANCE

Volga River

Dnieper River

Kiev

Black Sea   Caspian Sea

Byzantium

HEDEBY

Most Vikings lived as farmers, but specialist craftworkers such as blacksmiths, weavers, silversmiths, antler-carvers and carpenters preferred to live in towns, where they could sell their products. Viking towns were near the sea.

Hedeby in Denmark was an exceptionally big and flourishing Viking town. It was surrounded by thick, high walls of earth, which were entered by tunnels. There was also a strong sea wall made of wood. Within these fortifications the merchants and craftsmen lived in wooden houses along stone-paved streets.

Merchants came from as far away as France, Russia, Spain and the Middle East. There was the usual trade in food and weapons, as well as pottery and cloth, and luxuries such as furs and spices. Hedeby was also an important slave market. Slavery was a fact of life in Europe and prisoners of war were sold to the highest bidder. Slaves owned by Vikings were known as thralls. Their owners had power of life and death over them and they were forbidden to bear arms.

In 1050 Hedeby was raided and burned by the king of Norway. There were no monks on hand to detail this event, but from the town's remains archaeologists have put together a complete picture of daily life in a busy Viking town. Whole ships were sunk in the harbor during the raid.

VIKING SILVER

Silver was highly valued and hoards of coins and silver objects have been found. At least 40,000 coins have been found in Sweden alone. In the days before banks wealthy people had to hide their valuables. The hoards were abandoned when the owners died before passing on their secrets.

GROWING UP

From an early age Viking children were taught to help adults. When the men were off a-viking, the women managed the farms. Some Viking women were farmers and traders in their own right. Girls had to be trained to run a household. They also had to become expert spinners and weavers so they could make clothes, ship sails, cargo bags, wagon-coverings, wall hangings and blankets. Although all marriages were arranged between families, couples could separate.

Before they were old enough to sail with the men, boys had to learn how to plow straight furrows and cut wood. Some of their work, especially hunting, fishing and boat building, would have been fun.

Little children played with model boats and wooden swords and farmsteads modeled out of clay. The Vikings liked all kinds of outdoor ballgames. In winter ice-skating and skiing were popular outdoor activities. Indoors children could hear stories of Viking adventures and play board and dice games.

A VIKING HOUSE

The Vikings built houses of wood, when it was available, stone when it was not. The houses were thatched with reeds or straw or turf, out of which grass continued to grow. Viking families usually cooked, ate, worked and slept in one very big room with a raised fireplace in the middle.

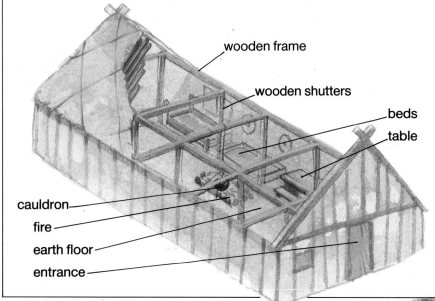

wooden frame

wooden shutters

beds

table

cauldron

fire

earth floor

entrance

As a mark of her authority a woman in charge of a household wore her keys on a chain dangling from one of her shoulder brooches. Though cozy, Viking houses must have been pretty smelly because there was only a small hole in the roof to let out smoke from the fire. The house was a center of activities, but there were also outbuildings which served as stables, barns, weaving or smithy workshops and bathrooms.

FARMING AND FISHING

The Vikings were very self-sufficient. They were hard-working farmers who could make almost everything they needed. They had fields of rye, barley, wheat and oats. These crops provided such everyday foods as porridge, bread and soups. Peas and beans were grown near the house, but other vegetables and nuts were gathered from the wild.

Hunting and fishing went on all year round. Apart from fishing in the sea, the Vikings used baited lines, traps and nets to catch salmon and trout in streams and lakes. Fish were dried on racks and then salted or smoked. Large sea mammals such as seals, walruses and whales were also hunted.

In summer sheep and cows were driven up to the rich mountain pastures. Then as winter approached some of them were slaughtered and their meat preserved by being salted or pickled. The salt was obtained by boiling seawater. Meat was roasted on a spit, stewed in a cauldron or cooked next to hot stones.

The whole family had to work on the farm. Thralls were slaves who worked on farms. Sometimes free born men, known as karls, who did not have any land of their own, worked on the land of wealthy farmers. There was plenty of work carrying water and collecting wood. Storing the food for the long winter was very important. Food was kept in larders. Butter was buried in tubs in the ground. Dried fish and meat could be hung on the outside walls of the house.

BONE AND ANTLER

The Vikings used bone and antler from the animals they hunted to make all sorts of everyday objects. The antlers from reindeer and deer were used to make combs (top left). Bone was used to make pieces for spinning wool (the circular objects in this picture) and pins and needles (in the center right). The other longer pieces were also made of bone and used for spinning. At the top right are fragments of Viking material.

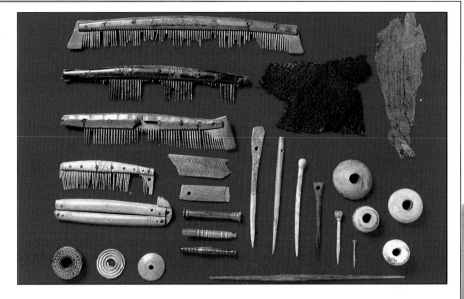

17

FEASTING

When they were far out at sea or isolated on their farms, the Vikings looked forward to their great feasts. At these holidays families were reunited, all the news and gossip was exchanged and weddings and deals were arranged. Not surprisingly the Vikings' idea of heaven was a permanent feast.

There were three major feasts in the year. The first took place after the winter solstice, after Christmas. The second took place in April and the third in mid-October celebrated the harvest. Before gathering in the big hall where the eating and drinking went on, the celebrators offered sacrifices to the gods. Animals and even men were killed. If it was the feast before summer, the gods would be asked for victory in the battles and raids to come. Outdoors, spectator sports probably took place with contests and races to show physical strength. All the people wore their finest clothes and their most precious jewels.

Everyone ate and drank themselves silly at a feast. The special meat eaten at the festivals was horsemeat. They drank beer, mead and, if they were wealthy, wine. Cattle horns provided drinking cups. Viking men were proud drunkards: "I leave no ale in the horn," boasted one hero, "though the warrior brings it to me until morning." Feasts were usually accompanied by entertainment in the form of poetry recitals and music.

RUNES

The borders of this casket have been decorated with runes. This was the Viking alphabet of letters made up of straight lines. Runes were easy to carve on wood, bone and even stone.

Vikings carved their names on personal things such as combs and gravestones, and on landmarks of places they visited. There were only 16 letters in the runic alphabet.

RELIGION

The Vikings did not build temples. Instead they worshipped their gods in the open air, choosing natural landmarks such as huge rocks, unusual trees or waterfalls.

The Vikings believed that there was life after death and that people would need earthly things in the afterlife. The most ordinary woman was buried with her cooking pot, some food and her favorite clothes. Wealthy people were buried with whole ship households. As well as food, clothes and furniture, dogs, horses and favorite slaves were killed to accompany their owners to heaven. Fortunately for archaeologists, many of the ships were buried under huge mounds rather than burned.

The Vikings who died in battle went to a special heaven. Odin sent warrior maidens called Valkyries to carry them off to the great hall known as Valhalla. They would spend the rest of their days there feasting and drinking. Knowing that Valhalla was their reward, Vikings soldiers showed great courage.

The Oseberg ship was discovered in Norway in 1903. The ship was probably built in 800 and buried in 850. It contained the skeletons of an old rheumatic woman and a very young woman. It is not clear whether the old woman was the servant of a princess, or the young woman was the slave maid of a queen. The ship contained three beds, four sleds, a beautiful four-wheeled cart, tapestries, chests, boxes, kitchen equipment, casks, looms, riding harness, and many other things, as well as the skeletons of at least ten horses and two oxen.

VIKING GODS

The tapestry shows Odin (with axe), Thor (with hammer) and Frey (with corn). Odin was the chief god. At dawn his two ravens, Hugin and Mugin, set out to fly all over the world and returned each night to report to him on what they had seen. He was very wise and concerned himself with magic and the dead. Thor was a happy-go-lucky character who made the noise of thunder with his great hammer, and was the mother goddess Frigg's son. Frey was the god in charge of all growing things, of peace and plenty. Frigg spun gold thread on her spinning wheel and it was woven into summer clouds. The gods expected sacrifices, which were made at the festivals. In exchange the gods were supposed to give good winters, harvests, and victories in battle.

GOVERNMENT

Family ties were very important to the Vikings. When they were away at sea, they needed someone to look after their money and land. The more land and treasure a man had, the more important he and his family were. Sometimes the family ties could lead to feuds between rival families lasting several generations. If one family member was killed, then his murderer had to be punished. A relative of the murdered man would kill the murderer or one of his relatives. These kind of disputes could also be sorted out at a "Thing."

The Thing was an open air meeting of all the freemen in the district. It met regularly to discuss problems and settled arguments about thefts, divorce, murder, and the ownership of land. Things worked both as law courts and governing bodies.

Iceland did not have kings. Instead the Althing met every summer at the Thingvellir, a great plain in front of a lava cliff. Sometimes quarrels at Things were settled by duels to the death. Some had to undergo ordeals to prove they were telling the truth. In Iceland, for example, women were asked to pick stones out of vats of boiling water. Their hands were bandaged for a time and then examined. If the wound was clean it was decided that they had been telling the truth.

Every man who owned property could vote but powerful, wealthy men had more of a say than the others. Larger, national Things met in the summer. These were great social occasions, where news was exchanged and business sorted out. Things could meet for several weeks so those who attended brought tents, cooking ware and goods to sell.

Most crimes were punished by banishment or fines. These had to be paid in public. If a banished man didn't leave, he could be lawfully killed. Erik the Red was outlawed by a Norwegian Thing, only to murder another man in Iceland. He was banished from there and sailed off to discover Greenland.

VINLAND

Around 860 a Swedish chieftain was blown by a storm to the coast of Iceland and by 930 there were about 50,000 people living at the new colony. In 982 Erik the Red sailed westwards from Iceland to find another large island, which he called Greenland. This island was cold with little good farming land, but to tempt settlers he gave it a pleasant name. Eventually about 3,000 people settled in Greenland. For food and profit they hunted whales, a very dangerous activity.

Erik the Red's son, Leif Erikson, discovered a place he called Vinland, the land of grapes. With its rich pastures and forests, North America seemed an ideal place to settle. Leif stayed in Greenland but others tried to settle Vinland. Among them was Gutrid, who had been shipwrecked before arriving in Greenland. In her ship, she brought sheep, cows and one bull.

Compared with Greenland, it was easy to survive in Vinland. The cattle could survive all year outside. At first the settlers got on very well with the North American Indians, who traded with them. But after a few years the settlers and the Indians became enemies and the Vinlanders had to sail away. Though some women, including Gutrid, had had babies, there were still too few settlers for Vinland to grow into a permanent colony. Gutrid returned to Iceland, became a Christian, and even made a pilgrimage to Rome. She ended her days as a nun.

For a long time people were not sure whether the story of Vinland was a myth or history, but in 1961 archaeologists found the remains of a Viking settlement at L'Anse-aux-Meadows in Newfoundland.

Although the Indians were frightened of the Vinlanders' enormous bull they enjoyed the taste of the milk from the settlers' cattle. The Indians were keen on some red cloth from Greenland. When stocks of the cloth ran low, the Indians exchanged the same numbers of skins and furs for smaller quantities of the cloth.

WHAT HAPPENED TO THE VIKINGS ?

After about 1066 the raiding stopped, and the Vikings began to lead more settled lives as townsmen and farmers. Powerful rulers established kingdoms in Norway, Sweden and Denmark, so life became more peaceful. Most important the Vikings were becoming Christians and trading took over from raiding.

It was also harder to launch raids. England, Ireland, Germany, Holland, and France now had strong armies to resist attacks. From 911 the northern shores of France were defended by the forces of a Danish chief called Rollo. He had been granted some land by the king of France as long as he did not attack other parts of France and defended it from other Vikings. The territory became known as Normandy and Rollo's followers were soon speaking French.

It was the same elsewhere. The first settlers kept in touch with their Scandinavian family. But once they became Christian and married into the local communities, it was difficult to tell the difference between the Vikings and the locals.

In 1066 William, the Duke of Normandy, landed in southern England. His armies defeated the English king and William and his followers seized English lands. He was descended from the Viking chief Rollo, who had married a local woman. William was so well settled in France that he and his followers were called Normans.

THE BAYEUX TAPESTRY

This part of the Bayeux tapestry shows the invasion of England by a Norman fleet. The ships used by William were not unlike the ones Rollo would have used. It shows that the Viking ship design was so good it lasted for several centuries. The tapestry was made by Norman women to commemorate the invasion. It gives us a good record of how William the Conqueror won. It is now kept in Bayeux in northern France.

27

VIKING TRACES

From the coins, weapons, jewelry and remains of houses, ships and towns, we know a great deal about life during the Viking Age. For other evidence of Viking influence we need only look at language. Thursday is "Thor's Day" and Wednesday is "Wodin's Day." Many English words to do with trading and sailing have Viking origins. Viking sailors would have understood the words stern and starboard. The word law is also a Viking word and out of their assemblies, the Things, modern-day legislatures have developed. Legislatures are where all the important decisions about running a country are made.

Many Viking settlements became important cities and towns. The Vikings chose places near the sea or on rivers with good trading possibilities. To them we owe Dublin and Kiev. Other cities, such as York in England, were taken over and expanded by Viking settlers so that they became important trading centers.

Here are some fishermen working off the Scottish coast. The islands of Orkney and Shetland were settled by the Vikings after 872. They were under Norwegian Viking control until as late as the 15th century. They retain many Viking customs.

UP HELLYA

On the last Tuesday in January the inhabitants of Lerwick, the capital of the Shetland Islands, celebrate the Up Hellya. This elaborate festival involves a lot of celebrating and feasting. A torchlit procession is followed by the setting on fire of a longboat. Some participants actually dress up as Vikings and most people wear fancy dress.

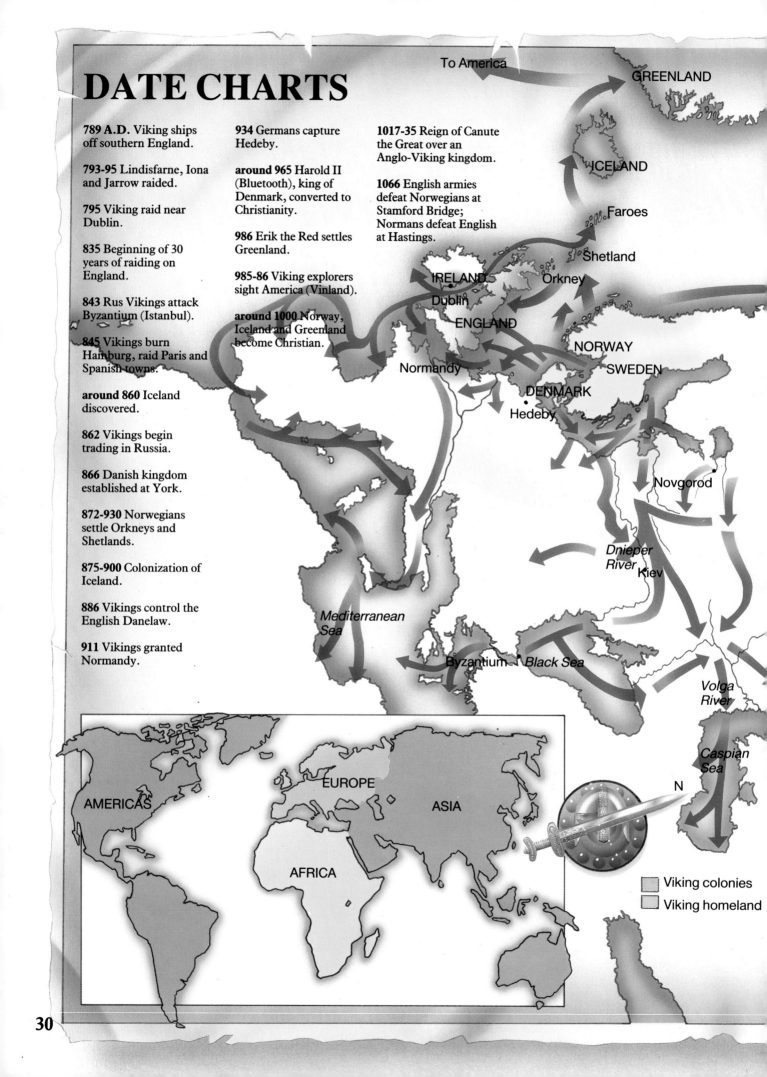

DATE CHARTS

789 A.D. Viking ships off southern England.

793-95 Lindisfarne, Iona and Jarrow raided.

795 Viking raid near Dublin.

835 Beginning of 30 years of raiding on England.

843 Rus Vikings attack Byzantium (Istanbul).

845 Vikings burn Hamburg, raid Paris and Spanish towns.

around 860 Iceland discovered.

862 Vikings begin trading in Russia.

866 Danish kingdom established at York.

872-930 Norwegians settle Orkneys and Shetlands.

875-900 Colonization of Iceland.

886 Vikings control the English Danelaw.

911 Vikings granted Normandy.

934 Germans capture Hedeby.

around 965 Harold II (Bluetooth), king of Denmark, converted to Christianity.

986 Erik the Red settles Greenland.

985-86 Viking explorers sight America (Vinland).

around 1000 Norway, Iceland and Greenland become Christian.

1017-35 Reign of Canute the Great over an Anglo-Viking kingdom.

1066 English armies defeat Norwegians at Stamford Bridge; Normans defeat English at Hastings.

To America

GREENLAND

ICELAND

Faroes

Shetland

IRELAND

Dublin

Orkney

ENGLAND

NORWAY

SWEDEN

Normandy

DENMARK

Hedeby

Novgorod

Dnieper River Kiev

Mediterranean Sea

Byzantium · *Black Sea*

Volga River

Caspian Sea

N

EUROPE

AMERICAS

ASIA

AFRICA

▢ Viking colonies
▢ Viking homeland

AFRICA	ASIA	AMERICAS	EUROPE
		600 A.D. onwards Late Classic period of the Mayan Empire.	
	618 A.D. Establishment of the T'ang dynasty in China.	**650-900** Huastecan culture on Gulf coast of Mexico.	
641 A.D. Arabs take over Egypt and overrun North Africa.			
700 Arab traders set up trading settlements in East Africa. Coptic Christians in Ethiopia.			**711 A.D.** Arabs conquer Spain, except the Asturias.
			732 Battle of Poitiers: the Arabs are defeated in southern France.
	751 Arabs defeat Chinese in central Asia.	**750** Mayan Empire declines.	**790s** Viking raids begin.
800 Beginning of Kanem Empire in central Sudan.			**800** Charlemagne crowned.
850 The city of Great Zimbabwe built.			**840s** Dublin founded.
			851 Danish army winters in England.
			860s Swedish Vikings active in Russia; Vikings take over York.
	907 End of the T'ang dynasty in China.	**900** Beginning of Mixtec culture in Mexico.	**871-99** Reign of Alfred the Great over Wessex (west of England).
920-1050 Height of the empire of Ghana, West Africa.	**960** Sung dynasty reunites China.		**911** Rollo granted Normandy.
969 Fatamids conquer Egypt and found Cairo.		**980** Toltec capital set up at Tula (Mexico).	
1000s Beginning of the Yoruba Empire on the Niger.	**around 1000** Gunpowder invented in China.	**1000** Leif Erikson travels down the American coast.	**around 1000** Iceland becomes Christian.
	1037 Seljuk Turks invade Khorasian, Jurjan and Tabaristan.		**1014-35** Reign of King Canute.
1054 Ghana conquered by the Almoravid Berbers from the north.	**1055** Entry of Tughril Beg into Baghdad where he is proclaimed sultan.		**1066** English defeat Norwegians at Stamford Bridge; Normans defeat English at Hastings.
	1071 Seljuks defeat Byzantines.		**1079-81** El Cid's campaigns against Moorish kingdom of Toledo in Spain.
			1080 King of Norway converted.
			1096 The First Crusade.

INDEX

Photographic Credits
The publisher would like to thank the Jorvik Centre/York Archaeological Trust for providing illustrative reference material for this book.
Pages 12, 18 and the back cover: Michael Holford; page 17: The York Archaeological Trust; page 21: Werner Forman Archive; page 27: Mary Evans Picture Library; page 29: David Simson/ Shetland Tourist Organisation.